the drive to win

Tide

10

HEART OF A
CHAMPION

dedicated to

all people with

THE *Drive*
TO WIN

HB
HONOR
BOOKS

The Drive to Win

ISBN 1-56292-847-3
Copyright © 2001 VisionQuest Communications Group, Inc.
and Koechel Peterson & Associates

Published by Honor Books
P.O. Box 55388
Tulsa, Oklahoma 74155

Research, Information, and Transcripts: Mary Ann Van Meter
and Annette Glavan

Text Editing: Lance Wubbels and John Humphrey

All quotes from current drivers are taken from interviews conducted
for various VisionQuest programs and projects.

This book in its entirety is the creation of Koechel Peterson & Associates
and VisionQuest Communications Group, Inc.

Photography by Tom Henry *(unless otherwise noted)*

Other photos listed here:
Pages 26-27,50-51 Robert LaBerge /ALLSPORT
Pages 28-29 Jay Sailors /AP
Pages 30-31 Andy Lyons /ALLSPORT
Pages 32,33 George Teidemann /TIMEPIX
Pages 32-33 Jamie Squire /ALLSPORT
Pages 50-51 Chris Stanford /ALLSPORT

FOREWORD

I've seen just about everything there is to see. I was there in the '70s when Richard Petty and Cale Yarborough turned racing into a true spectator sport. I was there in the '80s when network television entered the picture. I was there in the '90s when racing emerged from a backwoods hobby to become a national phenomenon. And now, in the beginning of a new millennium, I'm here to see racing become the new "sport of kings."

I've been at the top and the bottom. I've been the racing circuit's most hated and most popular driver. I've been a part of great teams, seen lots of checkered flags, and met thousands of fantastic people. I've been carried out in an ambulance and done the "Ickey Shuffle" in victory lane. I've been blessed to be a part of it all.

While I have seen incredible changes during my nearly thirty years in this sport, one thing has never changed—the drive to win. It fuels us all.

I started racing at the age of twelve. Forty years later, my reason for sitting behind the steering wheel was the same—I was driven to win. Without that incentive, I would never have experienced all those great racing moments.

There was a time when taking the checkered flag was all I cared about—success at any price. But everything changed a few years back when I found a better way—a victory beyond any racing experience I'd known. It gave me a new sense of purpose.

The men quoted in this book have discovered the same truth. They are true champions. They have risen above the challenges of the track and set a new standard for their lives. It was a privilege to race against them, and now, it's a thrill to report on them.

These men demonstrate how faith, courage, and determination can fuel us with a new drive to win, allowing us to overcome the wrecks, flat tires, and empty gas tanks that sidetrack us in life. They prove that winning on the track no longer defines who we are, and we have a new standard for success. It is the drive to win with God.

DARRELL WALTRIP *Winston Cup Champion 1981, '82, '85*
Racing Analyst, FOX Sports

"Hearing the sound of the roaring engines and seeing the speeds, everybody says, 'Boy, I'd like to go out there on a racetrack and run those types of speeds.' I think all of us have a little racer in us somewhere deep inside."

JEFF GORDON

RACE DAY
The Drive to Win

On asphalt battlegrounds from Daytona to California, a modern-day gladiator has emerged. Within great ovals thronged by hundreds of thousands of fans, veteran warriors with nerves and mounts of steel bask in the warmth of competitive fire. In these arenas, it is all about challenge and desire—defy the odds, conquer fear, cheat death, and live to drive again. Whether viewed from the safety of a grandstand seat or at the reins of 700-plus horses, it's clear the fastest-growing sport in America is here to stay.

In the sport of stock-car racing, life behind the wheel or in the pits is indeed life on the edge. A slip, a lapse in concentration, a blown pit stop, or an improper mechanical adjustment can mean disaster. Competition is fierce and sometimes heated. While forty-three cars line up at the start line each race day, only one captures the checkered flag. For the others—whether finishing second or forty-third—anything but a win means virtually nothing.

For the men and women of NASCAR—whether drivers or team members—it is the drive to win, a passion fueled by a force inside, that pushes them beyond their own abilities. On tracks across America, where paychecks and reputations are earned one day at a time, it is the formula that shapes champions.

But beyond the passion, this sport is also very much about family. The racing community itself seems immutably linked together. Love of the sport has been passed down from generation to generation. Sons wait their turn to fill shoes occupied by their fathers, who in turn sit in seats once filled by their fathers. Racing, it seems, is passed down more than hand-me-down clothes. Some people say it is simply in the blood.

From February to November, stock-car racing is also a life-style for the drivers, crews, and their families. The racing culture provides many opportunities for teams to partake in much together. Everything from meals to sponsor appearances to autograph sessions to chapel services are shared among competitors. The camaraderie provides balance and a system of support, creating an atmosphere where humanity will not be sacrificed for victory. No honorable driver will put an opponent at risk for the sake of self gain. Mutual respect abounds. Many pray together before going out on the track to compete.

A common heritage surrounds this ever-changing sport. In the good old days, the good old boys raced stock cars up and down Florida beaches, and names like Petty, Allison, Yarborough, and Jarrett were king. In the modern era,

"It's no different than football, baseball, whatever. Everything's got to work together to become number one in our sport."

BILL ELLIOTT

hundreds of thousands of spectators sit in multi-million-dollar state-of-the-art complexes to watch Gordon, Labonte, Earnhardt, and the Petty and Jarrett heirs. A decade from now, they will be watching a Jarrett and an Earnhardt of yet another generation in races held around the world.

Some names have changed over the years, as have the roles of the driver and the machines they steer. Race cars were once street cars souped up by drivers in home garages late at night. Today, the cars are incredible financial investments built completely from the ground up, equipped with huge, powerful engines, and tattooed with sponsor logos—fast-moving billboards. Now, they keep machinists and technicians up all hours trying to figure ways to coax extra hundredths of a second out of their 700-horsepower earthshaking machines.

Even the crowds have changed. While the faithful still come from small towns around the South, today's crowd is as diverse as those who walk a New York City street. Wall Street execs and construction workers, country and city folk, Ford truck and Mercedes Benz drivers, male and female, young and old—they all come to the track. In major metropolitan areas such as Southern California, Phoenix, Dallas/Fort Worth, Las Vegas, and Chicago, this sport has become a passion for those without racing roots and has grown far beyond what its innovators imagined. Commercialism and capitalism are as prominent at the tracks as cookouts and campers.

Though much has changed about this once backwoods hobby, stock-car racing is still motivated by one thing. On the track or in life, these modern-day charioteers are driven to be the best. They long to lap the competition; they will to walk away from each collision; and they love to go fast.

"The sport's just grown up. The first race we ever went to, we drove the race car to the racetrack.

Now we've got $500,000 trucks and trailers that take them into the racetrack. Initially, it was strictly

stock car. They took the muffler off, the headlights out, put a number on it, and ran it.

Now they're all-out racers. They look like street cars from the outside, but inside they're strictly race cars."

RICHARD PETTY

"I've been racing ever since I was twelve years old, so that tells you how long I've been going around and around and around. Sometimes I think I ought to go around and around the other way and see if I can unwind a little bit."

DARRELL WALTRIP

The men quoted in this book also strive to stand as examples of character and virtue. Each one is driven by a force inside that pushes him to become something greater than he could become by himself. They are driven to excellence and to make an impact on others. They are family men of faith and conviction, who are friendly with their fans, approachable, likable, and vulnerable. Having endeared themselves to a willing public, they stand as true examples of virtue.

To them, the drive to win means more than just pushing a car to victory lane. It's also about dealing with the wrecks on the track and the crashes in life and walking away from them as better human beings. And it's a matter of the drive to influence others. This is the true drive to win.

These men inspire us to let that same force drive us beyond adversity and our own limitations to reach the ultimate winner's circle.

"It's addictive. I can't imagine doing anything else."

ROBERT PRESSLEY

"The sport has become so popular and has

really changed. This is the greatest time in history

to be a part of NASCAR racing, and I'm

lucky enough I got a piece of it."

MARK MARTIN

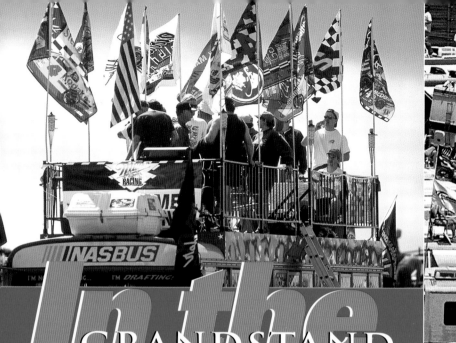

In the
GRANDSTAND

Sunglasses are in. Earplugs are a necessity . . . if you'd like to hear anything at all in the hours following the race. In the best seats in the house, you'll feel the hair on the back of your neck and the top of your head stand up and blow in the draft of forty-three cars as they fly past. Attached to thousands of ears are not transistor radios, but rather radio scanners. With these, avid fans can eavesdrop on the ongoing conversations between the driver of choice and his crew.

"Our sport is very unique in the way that kids and adults are
able to get close to the figures that they see racing on TV.
Not only do they get to meet us, but, in some cases,
we get to help make a positive impact on their lives."

DALE JARRETT

"Racing is my platform, it's my stage, and that's where I do my performing. So whatever I've done in my career, I've always used racing as my backdrop."

DARRELL WALTRIP

Seemingly overnight, stock-car racing has moved out of the shadows to become today's top spectator sport. There is something remarkably alluring about a raceway, something magical that draws people in and then continually draws them back. Hundreds of thousands of fans trek across the country to hit Winston Cup weekends. From remote locations such as the Poconos to sprawling metropolitan areas like Southern California, tracks have become veritable meccas for racing faithful making the weekly pilgrimage.

But the true stock-car fan is unlike that of any other sport. He or she is fiercely dedicated to his or her driver and unabashedly proud to display such devotion. Whether it is Gordon, Earnhardt, Wallace, or Martin, NASCAR fans gladly stand by their man. They come decked out in cap, shirt, and jacket displaying the likeness, signature, and number of their heroes. Stickers adorn their bumpers, and banners fill the windows of their campers, trucks, and motor homes. For some, it's a newfound obsession. For others, it's a way of life. To them, all other drivers are either bystanders or enemies.

For true racing fans, the infield is the only place to be on race weekend. The procession begins on Wednesday night as a steady stream of campers begins to fill the infield, settling in prime real estate. License plates from North Carolina, Georgia, South Carolina, Tennessee, Florida, and Kentucky stand side by side. Barbecue grills and lawn chairs clutter the landscape. Portable televisions declare the favorite for Sunday's race, while on every acre men and women gather by the hundreds to share the smell of grilled meat, the taste of a cold drink, and their favorite racing stories.

For them, this is more than just a race. It is an event, an experience—akin to an outdoor festival. It is fellowship, entertainment, and memories all built into one glorious weekend, until they do it all again the following week.

They are friendly in the infield, but once in the grandstand, it's clear where their loyalties lie, as evidenced by the cacophony of cheers and boos that rain down during driver introductions. To some, criticism of their "favored one" is just short of being fightin' words.

But here, too, it is like one big extended family—debating, laughing, hugging, arguing—enjoying their weekly version of a reunion. It is these people who make racing the spectacle it is.

"I was the most unpopular driver in the sport. People hated me. They called me 'Jaws.' They booed me. A guy came down from the stands one day; his hat was torn—you could tell it had been sliced with a knife. He looked at me and said, 'I'm going to tell you something, it's tough being a Darrell Waltrip fan in this sport.' That was my image. From 1983 on, I made a conscious, one-hundred-percent effort to turn that around. And in 1989, six years later, I was the most popular driver in the sport. I'm not anywhere near the same guy I was then, and it's because of my relationship with our Savior."

DARRELL WALTRIP

RACING TERMINOLOGY

PUSHING when the front end of the car and front tires are sliding.

TIGHT when the front tires do not hold the track in a turn because they lose traction before the rear tires. When this happens, the car will go straight even though the driver is turning the steering wheel. This is typically the cause of the front end of the car hitting the wall.

LOOSE when the rear of the car slides out and starts to fishtail in a turn, making the driver feel as though the rear end of the car will slide forward and he will lose control. When this happens, often the rear end of the car will hit the wall.

WEDGE OR CROSS the weight differential between the left front to right rear of the car and the left rear to right front of the car.

RUBBER an apparatus that is placed inside a spring to strengthen a particular part of the car. When the car is tight, a rubber will be placed in the right rear of the car to provide more freedom. A rubber will be placed in the left front of the car to help give sharper turns.

SPOTTER a team member who watches the race from high in the grandstands and relays information for the driver on where to go on the track to avoid an accident or pass another car.

TRAIL BRAKING tapping the brakes as the driver goes through a turn.

DRAFTING when a driver pulls up behind the car in front of him and uses that car as a shield from the air draft. This conserves fuel and allows the driver behind an opportunity to pick his spot to pass the car in front.

BUMP DRAFTING when one car comes up behind another, drafts behind him, then bumps him to move around and ahead of him. Dale Earnhardt has been credited as the technique's creator.

GETTING HUNG OUT TO DRY when a driver loses his draft position and is falling back in the pack.

HAT DANCE after the race, when the winning driver must put on the baseball cap of each of his sponsors for photos and television.

SPOT
SPOTLIGHT

The noise is deafening as mighty engines pound on eardrums like the man with the big bass drum in a marching band. Gas fumes fill the air like the smell of napalm on China Beach. The atmosphere is thick of both festival and conflict and is pulsing with anticipation. The roar from a sea of rabid fans can be a driving force for the NASCAR driver.

More than six million spectators will come to the tracks this year, with another two hundred million watching on television. Armed with a four-hundred-million-dollar-television contract and new multi-million-dollar racing complexes under construction in the western, central, and northern parts of the United States, stock car racing headed into the new millennium as the fastest-growing spectator sport in the world. Drivers have become icons. Merchandise sales have skyrocketed. And fan interest continues to boom. With all that have come greater expectations.

"You can hardly go anywhere without being recognized anymore. But I think that's good, because as athletes we accept the responsibility to be role models."

DALE JARRETT

"Now the driver is in the limelight constantly. He has to be very aware of what he says and what he does."

NED JARRETT

"The spotlight is so hot it almost burns sometimes."

MARK MARTIN

"It's certainly been overwhelming, and I think it takes time to learn how to handle it. But any time it gets difficult, or I say, 'Boy, I need to get out of this situation,' I just think how fortunate I am, and it puts things in perspective."

JEFF GORDON

In the early days, the driver focused on two things—driving the car and getting it ready for the race. Today, the requirements are much more intensive, the pressures more weighty. Today's stock-car driver is part expert behind the wheel and part corporate pitchman. He has to perform not only on the track but also in the boardroom. He must be as skilled in dealing with the media, autograph sessions, and promotional opportunities as he is at going into a turn at 180 miles per hour.

The pressure is intense. Lose on the track and you fall back in the points race. Lose a sponsor and you may not have a ride next week.

For the driver, it is imperative to keep everything in perspective. But with the incredible explosion of the sport's popularity, the increasing intensity of the spotlight has caused growing pains.

"Along with the growth have come bigger sponsors, more media, more responsibility, and more pressure on the driver to go out and perform—on the racetrack, in the boardroom, signing autographs. . . . It's an all-inclusive package now."

KYLE PETTY

700 HORSES

Seven-hundred-plus horsepower of brute speed and handling packed into 3,400 pounds. Five quarts of hot oil course through its rubber veins as it devours twenty-two gallons of gasoline at the less-than-economical rate of four miles per gallon. Stuffed under the hood you'll find a V-8 small block engine that displaces between 350 and 358 cubic inches, running at 8,600 rpm, using a carburetor instead of fuel injection, and costing around $80,000.

There are no store-bought parts in this baby. It is custom-built from the ground up. And the mechanical and engineering teams are always working on manufacturing new parts and ways to get an edge.

Its tires are changed like a baby's diapers, but this set of Pampers runs around $1,300. There are no headlights or brake lights. No doors or trunk. No speedometer, horn, or gas gauge. No driver's-side window. No plush leather interior. And no air conditioning.

It is sleek, low to the ground, very loud, and very fast.

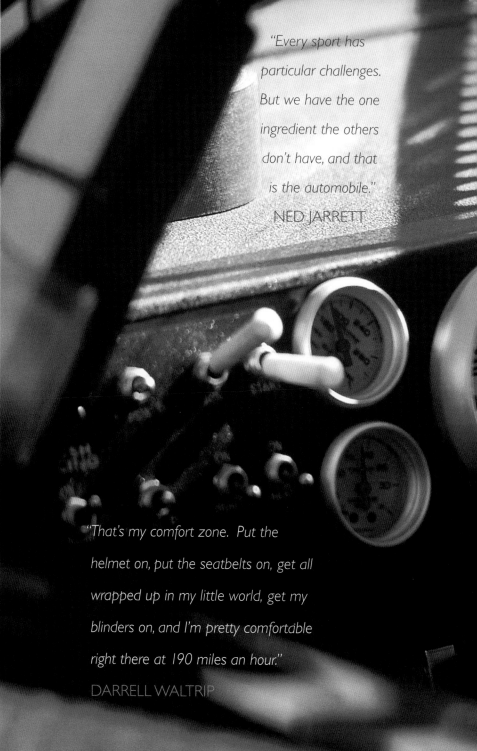

"Every sport has particular challenges. But we have the one ingredient the others don't have, and that is the automobile."

NED JARRETT

"That's my comfort zone. Put the helmet on, put the seatbelts on, get all wrapped up in my little world, get my blinders on, and I'm pretty comfortable right there at 190 miles an hour."

DARRELL WALTRIP

"With temperatures reaching upwards to 150 degrees, we don't have the opportunity to call a time out or say 'I need a drink of water' or 'I want to come out of the game for a little while.' We have to go at it continuously for four to four-and-a-half hours."

DALE JARRETT

"The radial tires with power steering, the speeds, the aerodynamics, and the high-bank tracks take a toll on you after a five-hundred-mile race. Just get in your car, turn your radio wide open, turn the heater wide open, and then drive down the road in bumper-to-bumper traffic for three-and-a-half hours, and see what your mental state is at the end of the day."

DARRELL WALTRIP

This is the stock car. Over the past several decades, it remains the object of desire and the subject of awe for many men and women.

Driving this monster in a race is clearly not like a Sunday cruise along the parkway. It is an all-out attack on one's senses—the highest levels of stress, heat, noise, discomfort, and G forces. It is four hours of shake, rattle, and roll. No food, no rest stops, no time outs, no bathroom breaks, no stretching your legs. The floorboards and pedals get so hot that drivers wear heat shields on their feet. Some even cut out the bottoms of Styrofoam cups and attach them to their heels. To make it through is a sheer test of endurance.

With all the inherent displeasures, it is still the one thing that will continue to set this sport apart from any other. America always has had, and always will have, a special love for fast cars.

"The part I like most is physically being in the car, physically driving the car. I can't think of anything else I'd rather do. That's my passion."

KYLE PETTY

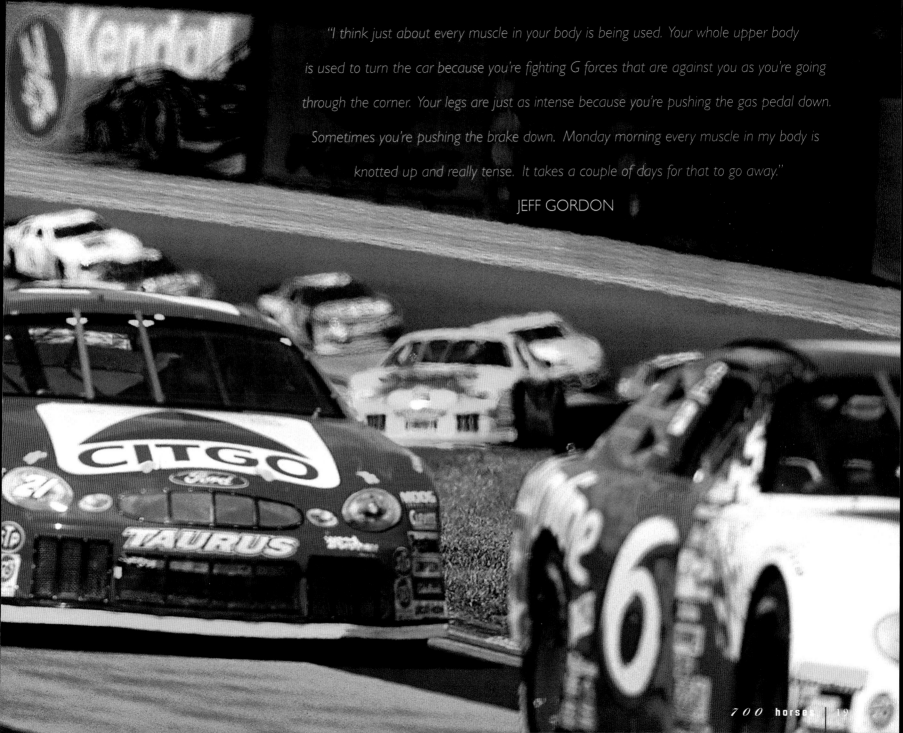

"I think just about every muscle in your body is being used. Your whole upper body is used to turn the car because you're fighting G forces that are against you as you're going through the corner. Your legs are just as intense because you're pushing the gas pedal down. Sometimes you're pushing the brake down. Monday morning every muscle in my body is knotted up and really tense. It takes a couple of days for that to go away."

JEFF GORDON

"I loved driving a race car when I was very young. Five years old is when I first got behind the wheel of a race car. I was gung-ho on just about anything that had wheels and went real fast. I loved it from the start."

JEFF GORDON

ROAD WARRIORS

The man who sits behind the wheel is a different breed . . . a dichotomy of emotions. Composed yet teeming with nervous energy. Aggressive but patient. Pensive and fearless. Risking but controlled. Totally focused ahead yet keenly aware of everything around him.

He is the man in the steel cockpit. In his hands he holds 3,400 pounds of raw power . . . and his own destiny. He is capable of moving at speeds up to 200 miles per hour and is always a split second away from inexorably altering his future. For the driver, racing is not merely a hobby, a job, or a passion. It is his life.

"When I first started, a driver had to pace himself. The driver was much tougher than the car, so you had to finesse the car and pace yourself and not tear your car up or wear it out. The professional stock-car driver is more like a guy that runs a marathon. You train more like you're going to run a twenty-six-mile marathon. In the corner of the shop you'll see all the workout equipment. Part of the performance of the car is directly related to how good a shape the driver's in."

DARRELL WALTRIP

"To me what's important is to be able to go to a lot of different types of racetracks and conquer at different styles and different size tracks. Then you are universal, and that wins championships."

JEFF GORDON

"I take a couple of aspirin before the start of a race and try to take a couple of aspirin to limit my headaches at the end of a race. I try not to miss the drivers' meeting, go to our church service, then get back into that game face. There's a lot of mental in this."

RANDY LAJOIE

The constant threat of danger lurks around every turn and down each straightaway. In the blink of an eye, the NASCAR driver is forced to make life-or-death decisions, near impossible maneuvers, and accurate readings on the machine he is harnessing.

It is a role that can be immensely gratifying and equally thankless. Yet for each of these road warriors, it is all about the ride. The ride provides an adrenaline rush unlike any other.

And it's about the challenge. To go two wide, plunging into a turn, and see who can be first to edge the other car out in a high-speed game of "chicken" . . . just before hitting the wall. To turn an average car on a bad day into a top-five finish. To move from the back of the pack to the front, passing twenty-some cars along the way. And to have an even better finish next week.

"On race morning, you're butterflies.
Then once that engine cranks, the pain usually leaves you."
ROBERT PRESSLEY

"I have confidence in myself that I can go out there and drive the car, but I'm always trying to get better and improve on my driving. How to be a smarter driver but still be aggressive, how to communicate more or better with my race team. I always try to improve."
JEFF GORDON

"I've been in the car many a day in the driveway (as a kid) having my own races and dreaming of one day winning the Daytona 500. I'm one of the fortunate ones whose dreams came true."
DALE JARRETT

Tracks differ in what they present to the drivers. Some are flat-out pedal-to-the-medal superspeedways. Others are road tracks with numerous back and forth turns, testing the driver's skill and ability to maneuver his machine. Some are short tracks. Some provide for two- and three-wide racing, but other tracks make that prospect much too risky.

Drivers must cope with the midday heat of Texas, the late fall chill of Atlanta, the mist of the Poconos, and Saturday-night lights. Road conditions, surfaces, and competitors can vary drastically from week to week. All these must be conquered while keeping the emphasis on speed.

It is the drive to win that fuels the driver's will to compete and spurs him to find ways to overcome each week's challenges. And it is the sheer love for the sport—man and machine—that, for the driver, makes it all pure joy.

"You can't have your mind wander. You've got to be 110 percent focused on what you are doing."

DARRELL WALTRIP

SPEED SPEED SPEED

SPEED

SPEED

"Racing is controlled excitement at a very fast pace."

DAVID GREEN

Blazing down a straightaway at 200-plus miles per hour and barreling into a turn at 160 is a thrill like no other. The racer's senses are heightened as G forces shove him back into his seat. The car moves in and out of a turn in a heartbeat. Images outside the car are an optical blur. Yet time seems to stand still. Endorphins release in the driver's brain like a fine rain shower. The adrenaline rush reaches a stage of full flow, and the driver is on a "high" that no other experience can ever imitate. It goes beyond even the ultimate super-fast roller coaster with the unexpected around every turn.

Drivers experience the rush of controlling speed one moment and being completely at its mercy in the next. It's the double-edged sword of feeling as though you've mastered a two-hundred-miles-per-hour machine while knowing you really ultimately cannot.

The thrill they experience at ultra-high speeds on a superspeedway is the same type they knew as a sixteen-year-old, foolishly pushing a 1976 Camaro to 105 miles per hour on a remote desert road, or as a nine-year-old, running a mini-street dragster to a junior title. It's the adrenaline rush—there from the first day they sat in something with four wheels and an engine—that makes this experience unique to the sport.

Speed is the element that unites all drivers. A love of it can fuel the drive to win. A respect for it separates them from the pretenders.

"...maybe being in an airplane that's out of control—the kind of thrill, the kind of fear like a roller-coaster ride when you come up over the top: you wonder if there's any bottom or not. A car that's going entirely too fast for the conditions, those are the feelings you have."

DARRELL WALTRIP

"It feels fast if there's a car that's not running very fast and you go by it. That's when you feel the speed."

ERNIE IRVAN

"It'll get your attention when you go down in the corner like we do. It's one of the greatest feelings and rushes that I know of."

BOBBY LABONTE

"We race these cars inches apart at 200 miles an hour."
MARK MARTIN

"Having started when I was thirteen, I've always gone fast. If I felt like I was going 200 miles per hour, I'd probably get scared and want to do something else. You're just trying to go faster than the guy in front of you."
LAKE SPEED

"In our sport, you get used to speed. Once you start getting used to the speed of running over 150 or 160 miles an hour, from 190 to 215 there's hardly any difference."

"I love to go fast."
STEVE GRISSOM

BILL ELLIOTT

"People ask all the time about driving on the highway. Well, I don't drive fast there. I get my thrill out here. And it is a tremendous thrill to go this fast."
DALE JARRETT

On the EDGE

From the eye of the spectator, the line between fear and fascination becomes blurred. But at 200 miles per hour, the fears of the NASCAR driver exist on an entirely different plane. In the constant dance with danger, a minor error in judgment can produce unspeakable consequences.

Racing inches apart, drivers know a sudden problem with the car in front or beside them, an unforeseen move from a driver ahead in the pack, or a misjudged charge from behind can all affect them. Any one of these can result in a multi-car pile-up, not unlike the accidents rubberneckers view on the side of the freeway. It is indeed sudden impact.

"Sometimes the car feels like you're driving really fast on a gravel road. It's kind of like you're under control, but you know you're really not under control ... you're just a little under control."

LAKE SPEED

"Every time that you step in there, anything can happen."

BOBBY LABONTE

"I race hard. I know I might crash from time to time. I'm as sure as anything that I'll never get hurt in an accident where I'm in control of the car. But there's a lot of situations where you become a passenger, not a driver. I don't want to die. I'm not ready to leave yet. I desperately want to be a part of my son growing up and being a good husband to my wife. I don't want all that to end."

MARK MARTIN

"When you really know how fast you're going is when you're headed the wrong way."

RANDY LAJOIE

"A wreck takes forever to happen. We're talking tenths of seconds from the time you know you're going to wreck until it happens, and it seems like it's an eternity."

ROBERT PRESSLEY

"Love overcomes fear. I love what I do and because I love what I do so much, the fear is overcome by the love of what I do."
DARRELL WALTRIP

"I think of being on the edge, just totally on the edge of out-of-control, yet still keeping it under control."
JEFF GORDON

"You always think that somebody may wreck, but today it's not going to be me. Anyone who tells you they're not afraid at some point in time in a race car, they're not telling you the truth. There's a healthy amount of fear in everybody out there. There are a lot of brave guys out here, but there are no crazy guys out here. Brave men are always fearful men."
KYLE PETTY

"I think that fear is what keeps you within that edge. I wouldn't feel comfortable starting the race without a good prayer."
JEFF GORDON

"I do say a prayer every time I go out in a race car. I just say, 'Lord, here's my life. This is what I do. I'm turning it over to You. Protect me while I do it.' I don't come back because I'm a great race car driver. I come back because He guides me back. When I look in the right side of a race car, there's Jesus hanging on to the roll bars right there beside me, and I have no fear then."
KYLE PETTY

For the NASCAR driver, danger is an ever-present reality, fear an unseen companion. Every driver on the track knows the next race could very well be the last. A clip from a passing car, a stuck throttle, or a worn tire can send him into the wall in a flash. Despite roll cages, helmets, fire-resistant suits, heavy-duty suspension, and safety nets, history has proven that the wall can be an unforgiving foe.

All of the drivers talk about hitting the wall. While it is the last thing they want to think about on race day, it is frequently foremost in their thoughts. These men understand their own mortality. They know that in a confrontation with the wall, they are never the winners.

But NASCAR drivers know danger is simply a built-in reality of what they do. Each has counted the cost before he straps himself into a seat.

On race day, before the blare of "Gentlemen, start your engines" is sounded, an eerie silence befalls the track. Chaplains from Motor Racing Outreach walk up and down pit row, praying with and for all forty-three drivers and their wives, one after another. None prays for victory. All pray for safety.

These men know the siren named fear will continuously call them, longing to remain their companion, their partner in this dance against death. Those who are fueled by the drive to win understand they must never stop listening to that siren's song.

There's no foolish bravado here. These men are well aware that a healthy dose of fear keeps them on the edge . . . and not beyond.

"I was in a huge accident—
not really hitting anything, just
spinning all around. My crew couldn't
see me. My crew chief asked me
on the radio, 'Did you get through
it, Mark?' My answer was, 'Can't
talk, still wrecking.' ".

MARK MARTIN

"You don't want to be
fearless, but you
want to be able to
go out there and run
fast. You've got to have
a little bit of fear in you
to get to that point."

BOBBY LABONTE

JUST THE FACTS

1949 Jim Roper wins the first NASCAR Strictly Stock (now Winston Cup) race at Charlotte, North Carolina Speedway.

1950 Darlington Raceway, the circuit's oldest track, opens in South Carolina.

1951 The first Winston Cup race run under lights is held at Columbia, South Carolina Speedway.

1959 Lee Petty wins the first Daytona 500.

1963 Fred Lorenzen becomes the first driver to pass the $100,000 mark in seasonal earnings.

1970 Buddy Baker becomes the first driver to break the 200-miles-per-hour average barrier with a lap of 200.47 during testing at Talladega, Alabama.

1979 The Daytona 500 is the first major Winston Cup race to have complete television coverage. Richard Petty wins the race.

1984 Richard Petty captures his 200th and final career win at Daytona. He retires as the sport's all-time leader in victories.

1985 Bill Elliott wins the first ever Winston Million.

1987 Bill Elliott sets the Winston Cup qualifying record with a speed of 212.809 miles per hour at Talladega.

1992 Lowe's Motor Speedway in Concord, North Carolina, becomes the first superspeedway to install lights and begin night racing.

1992 Richard Petty runs his final race in the same event in which Jeff Gordon makes his debut.

1994 Indianapolis Motor Speedway hosts the first ever Brickyard 400. Jeff Gordon wins.

1999 Tony Stewart wins three Winston Cup races, which is the most ever for a rookie.

"I like to see him on the track. I like to hear him on the radio and know what's going on. That's my lifeline. If I lose contact where I can't hear him, it's a little nerve-wracking to me. If I hear his voice on the scanner, I'm good. I'm really good."

PATTIE PETTY

nascar WIVES

"If you get out of there in first or twenty-first place, it doesn't matter. If you get out of there without a wrecked race car, it's a success. We're enjoying it for the moments that we're here because it will come and it will go. And so with that you have to build your life around other things besides just racing."

KELLEY JARRETT

The sport's danger is clearly not lost on the drivers' wives. With a steely disposition, these women travel from track to track with their husbands, always in a tug of war with their nerves.

Sunday mornings begin in a similar manner. Most wives attend the drivers' chapel service at the track with their husbands. They walk them out to pit row, whispering encouraging words along the way. Some tape handwritten prayers or Bible verses on the steering wheel. Then they pray with their husbands, kiss them, strap them into the cars, hopefully say, "I'll see you after the race," and release them into the hands of their crews and God. Then they simply walk away and trust both.

Wives deal in different ways with the harsh reality of a sport that too often leaves their peers without husbands. Some watch the race from the pits. Some stand atop team trailers to get the bigger picture. Others gather in a camper and watch the race on television, drawing strength from one another. Still others sit in the solitude of their own campers, choosing not to watch at all.

For the wives of NASCAR drivers, Sunday afternoons are an agonizingly long four hours of stomach churning, nail biting, praying, and waiting. When it's over, they send up a quick "Thank you, God," compose themselves, and waltz gracefully to meet their husbands at the garage or, for one blessed soul, in victory lane. On other days, some wives race to find their men at the infield hospital.

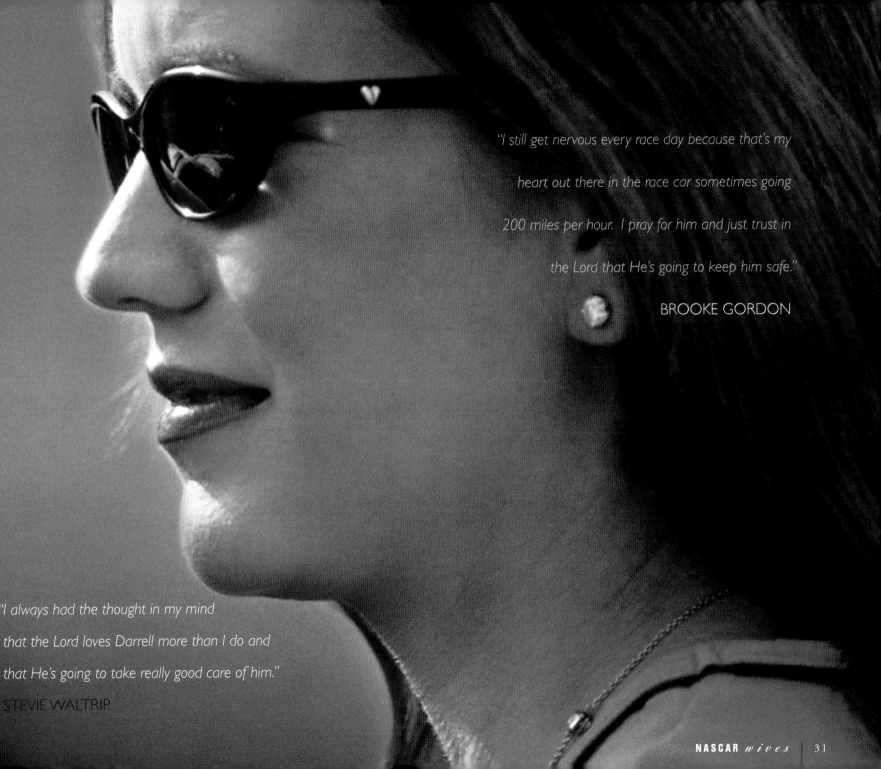

"I still get nervous every race day because that's my

heart out there in the race car sometimes going

200 miles per hour. I pray for him and just trust in

the Lord that He's going to keep him safe."

BROOKE GORDON

"I always had the thought in my mind

that the Lord loves Darrell more than I do and

that He's going to take really good care of him."

STEVIE WALTRIP

> *"It's a very scary feeling.*
>
> *You're on the edge with every turn*
>
> *and just constantly fearing the worst every lap."*
>
> LISA LAJOIE

> *"We have prayer before he gets in the car.*
> *I get to give him a little kiss and say, 'You're going to do well.*
> *We'll meet you in victory lane.' Then I usually walk back*
> *to the bus and find a place where I can watch the race*
> *by myself and stay in prayer a little bit."*
>
> PATTIE PETTY

> *"When he's running 190 miles an hour, I'm a little bit more*
> *nervous, a little bit more edgy. I have a lot of confidence*
> *in the cars and in his ability as a driver to use his head*
> *and not put himself in bad situations. But things happen,*
> *and that's where you depend on your faith. You start with*
> *a prayer, and you end with a thank-you prayer."*

KELLEY JARRETT

When an all-too-sudden quiet hits the track and the cars can be heard slowing down in mid race, a wife knows it can mean only one thing—an accident, perhaps catastrophe. It is then that the race in the mind begins. Dreaded questions run rampant circles around the tracks of her brain. Was it him? Is he alive? She prays as she rapidly hunts for the sight of her husband's car.

She looks at her child's face, which speaks without words, "Is it Daddy?" It is then she must muster all of her courage, strength, and faith and keep herself free from the encroaching panic. She is counselor, nurse, comforter, and encourager all wrapped into one. All in all, it is an emotional juggling act that requires great inner fortitude.

To survive, she has become accustomed to the full spectrum of emotional upheavals. She has learned to tolerate the love-hate relationship she has with racing. But most of all, she has learned to cherish every moment she has with her driver/husband.

"I've put scripture in my husband's car since the early '80s, and he'd stick it on the dash or somewhere he could see it."

STEVIE WALTRIP

"The night before the race, Jeff and I will look through the Bible and find a meaningful scripture. I'll put it on a little index card and tape it to his steering wheel. He tells me it helps him get that inner peace."

BROOKE GORDON

TEAM
TEAMWORK

"That's what really keeps me going and drives me ... working with the people on your team ... to move the car to the front of the pack and make great pit stops, communicate well, and then pull into victory lane together. That's the thrill I get."
JEFF GORDON

While drivers and their wives have learned the importance of working together, the team concept has been a part of stock-car racing since its earliest days. Crew members are the people who make the sport go. They don't care who gets the credit as long as the job gets done.

While a driver commands center stage and is a crucial component on any team, one man alone cannot make a team. It is far too easy to overlook the many crew members who form a race team. The driver is only as good as the teammates who support him behind the scenes, often unseen by the public eye. The main ingredient in stardom is the rest of the team.

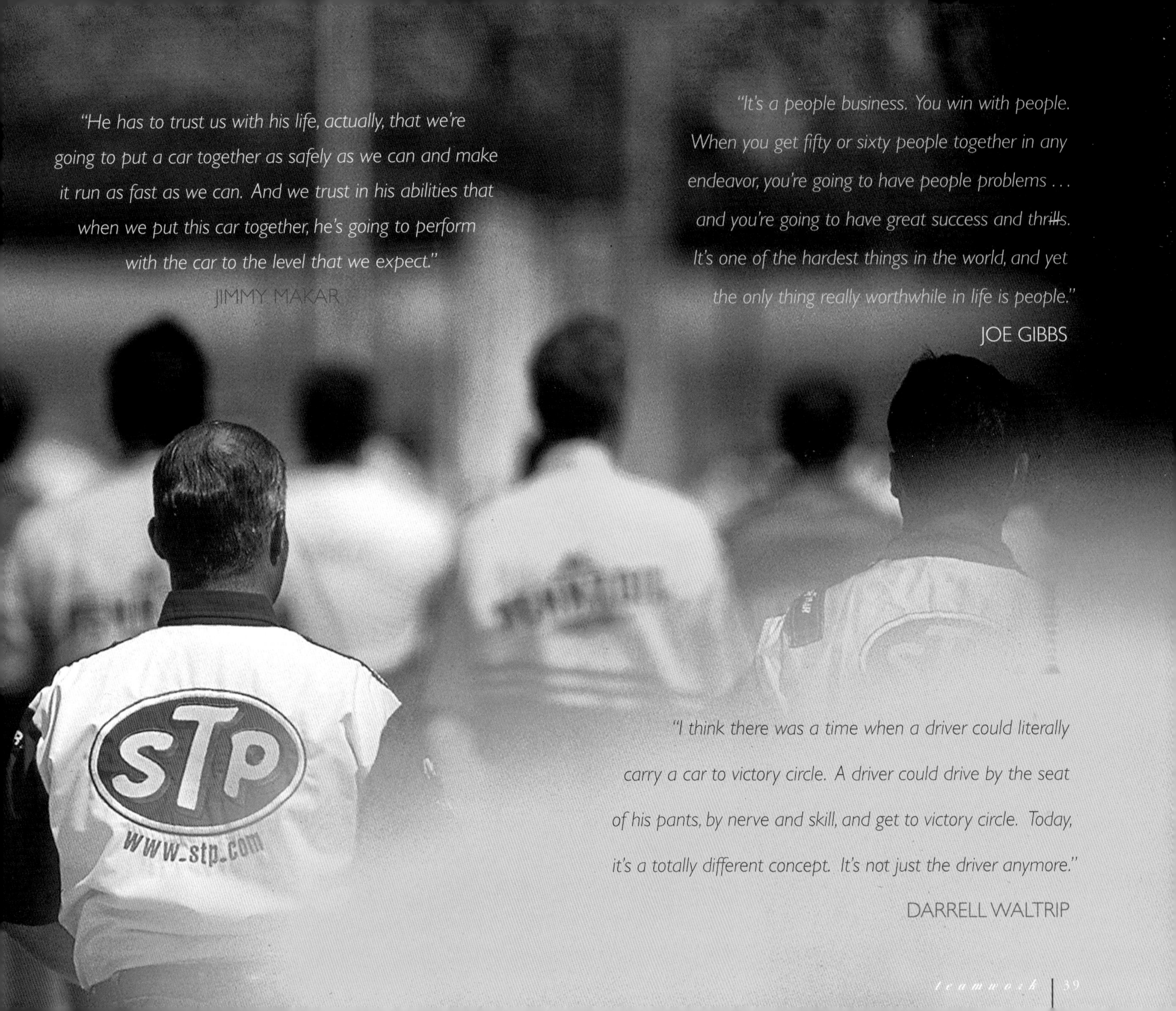

"He has to trust us with his life, actually, that we're going to put a car together as safely as we can and make it run as fast as we can. And we trust in his abilities that when we put this car together, he's going to perform with the car to the level that we expect."

JIMMY MAKAR

"It's a people business. You win with people. When you get fifty or sixty people together in any endeavor, you're going to have people problems . . . and you're going to have great success and thrills. It's one of the hardest things in the world, and yet the only thing really worthwhile in life is people."

JOE GIBBS

"I think there was a time when a driver could literally carry a car to victory circle. A driver could drive by the seat of his pants, by nerve and skill, and get to victory circle. Today, it's a totally different concept. It's not just the driver anymore."

DARRELL WALTRIP

PITS
IN THE PITS

"Nineteen, twenty, twenty-one seconds feels like forever. What three seconds is in the pits is probably like a man's average day."

ROBERT PRESSLEY

All sports are governed by the same principles. While football is a game of inches, racing is a game of seconds. Nowhere is this more evident than in the pits, where all stops are definitely not created equal.

Every pit stop is a test against time. It's a mental and physical challenge, all in the name of speed. It is here where races are won and lost.

"Every time you come on pit road, it can be a fire drill. A pit stop is a thing of beauty. I mean, it's like a ballet. You're sitting in the car and you see them go out. Tat, tat, tat, tat, tat. And you see them go back in. Tat, tat, tat, tat, tat. And you leave. Then there are other times when it's chaos. They go around and run into one another. The car falls off the jack. The guy's air wrench breaks. The can of gas in the back flies up in the air, and you're wondering if you're going to get out of there alive or not."

DARRELL WALTRIP

"A twenty-second pit stop is a terrible pit stop. Most of your competitors had eighteen-second pit stops. They automatically get out ahead of you."
ERNIE IRVAN

All sports are governed by the same principles. While football is a game of inches, racing is a game of seconds. Nowhere is this more evident than in the pits, where all stops are definitely not created equal.

Every pit stop is a test against time. It's a mental and physical challenge, all in the name of speed. It is here where races are won and lost.

The scene at a pit stop is like controlled chaos. Seven men leap over the wall and scurry around the car to change tires and replenish gasoline as quickly as possible. That's four new tires and twenty-two gallons of gas— in and out in 18 seconds and service with a smile.

"Everybody knows what the other guy is doing. I've got the gas can in my hands, and I step over the wall. The car stops, and after that it's all blacked out except for what I'm doing. I don't see the guy changing the tires. I don't see the cars going by. I'm just a part of the gear. The timing is so critical. We've got to beat these guys out or we're going to be way back on the racetrack."
DANNY "CHOCOLATE" MYERS

"It can seem like eternity.

You see all the other cars go and you're still on the jack.

It just seems like you're there forever."

STEVE GRISSOM

"You're leading the race, you come in the pits
and you make a 24-second pit stop. You know where
you're going to end up when you go back out on the track?
About 15th. You just took the fastest car, the best driver,
made a pit stop, and went from leading the race to 15th.
That's how critical teamwork is today."

DARRELL WALTRIP

"We've lost a few guys in the pits. We remember
those guys in our hearts and in our prayers,
but we don't talk about it. You can't think about whether
the car is going to hit you or catch fire, or whether the
guy behind you will stop. If we thought about it,
we couldn't do what we do."

DANNY MYERS

Pit crews are also masters of makeshift. If the driver scrapes the wall or is in a minor collision, someone has to take the tangled scraps of metal and quickly get the car back into running shape with some sense of aerodynamic efficiency. The pit crew springs into action like battlefield medics, trying anything to get the car back out on the track. Pull a damaged piece off here, expend a roll of duct tape there, and the heavily bandaged car is ready to go out into the fray again. It may not be pretty, but if the car can make it around the rest of the way, it can pick up valuable NASCAR Winston Cup points.

On tracks all across America, encased in the deafening solitude of his chosen trade, the NASCAR driver knows his success on a given Sunday is but a mere reflection of the people behind the wall. They live out their triumphs and failures together . . . and never give up.

"It's never ending when one's not going so well, but you realize these guys are giving everything they have. When they really go fast, it seems like you haven't been there but just a split second."

DALE JARRETT

Competition

COMPETITION

"You're racing forty-two guys, but you're not racing forty-two guys at one time. You race one guy. Once you pass him, the game changes and it's a new game, and you go again. It's the competition I like."

KYLE PETTY

While winning is the goal of every NASCAR team, the reality is that few ever see the checkered flag for themselves. Gordon, Martin, Jarrett, and Earnhardt seemingly fight for it every week. And behind them are a host of drivers who never pull to a stop in victory lane. There are drivers who have been racing for decades and still have trophy cases with lots of empty space.

What is it that drives these men who consistently finish at the back of the pack? It's the same thing that drives the champions—the love of the competition, the thrill of the ride, and the fact that come next Sunday, one of them just might be the man standing in the winner's circle.

To reach this level of competition, these drivers know how to drive fast. But it is a rare few who are set apart by their competitive hearts. The true test of a man's character comes when he is beset by roadblocks and it seems there is no possible way he can reach his destination . . . yet he keeps striving. The drive to win wills him to push on.

"We've never had the big bucks behind us or the big team that some have, but we've always been able to go out there and buck the odds. And when I outrun those guys, it gives me a lot more pleasure than it does for them to outrun me. I hope that my career will give a lot of other people hope that just because the odds are stacked against them, it doesn't mean they can't be victorious—whether it's in a career or in life."

LAKE SPEED

"There are forty-three great drivers out here,
and nobody's guaranteed anything. Some days are bad,
and we get banged up and maybe get a bruise or a broken bone.
But I've been able to walk away, then come back
and want to do it the next week."

DAVID GREEN

"I enjoy the challenge of trying to make my race
car better than everybody else's out there and for
a period of 400 or 500 miles being the best at it."

DALE JARRETT

"It doesn't matter whether I've qualified thirty-fourth or qualified
first. I'm still going to go run just as hard either way."

LAKE SPEED

It is in persevering against all odds that many drivers have become real-life heroes. These men are lauded not for talent alone but for their desire to keep going in the face of challenge. Many of them eagerly admit that it is the challenge itself that lights their competitive fire. It is the head-to-head competition with forty-two other men—one at a time—that makes them press on through and overcome fatigue, pain, and exhaustion and keep charging. Most will admit that it is the chase itself—overcoming the obstacles and finishing the race—that is enough to motivate them each week to push on in the pursuit of the other drivers, and ultimately to victory.

While his eyes are on the prize, the driver knows that winning cannot be his sole source of motivation. If it were, only a select few would stay in the race. But the desire to compete, the drive to conquer fear, the will to survive—the intangible characteristics pulled from deep down within—these continue to give him the drive to press on.

"You're running second, and somebody else is leading the race. He slips, you run first. Who cares? It only pays on the last lap."

KYLE PETTY

"We have to want to win. There's nothing like winning. I mean that. That's what it's all about, and that's what we're here for. That's what we do this for—the thrill of being out there competing."

STEVE GRISSOM

DID YOU KNOW?

- The site that now occupies Pocono Raceway was once a spinach farm.

- Dale Earnhardt was the first driver to win a race on radial tires in 1989.

- The admission fee to the first race at Darlington was five dollars.

- Kyle Petty once appeared on the television show *Hee Haw* as a singer.

- Richard Petty's car was put on display at the Smithsonian Institute.

- Current driver Dave Marcis has been known to drive while wearing wingtip shoes.

- Dale Earnhardt was the first stock-car driver to be pictured on a Wheaties cereal box.

- Curtis Turner was the first stock-car driver to appear on the cover of *Sports Illustrated* in 1957.

- In the 1999 Jiffy Lube 500, driver Jeff Burton won the race after starting from the 38th position. It was the second biggest come-from-behind victory in Winston Cup history, trailing only Johnny Mantz, who won the 1950 Southern 500 after starting 43rd.

- Richard Petty's 200 all-time NASCAR wins are the most ever. David Pearson is second with 105.

WINNER'S CIRCLE

In racing circles, the old axiom is true: "It's not how you start, it's how you finish." While the pole position is what every driver aims toward in the time trials, frequently it is a driver who started farther back in the pack who takes the checkered flag. Truly, where you finish is more important than where you start.

Many drivers see the metaphorical irony in their profession. While they focus on the immediacy, and sometimes monotony, of the race, they never lose sight of the prize before them. It is not the race itself that is all-encompassing; rather it is the finish.

"I've been very fortunate to be in victory lane. There are a lot of drivers who come through here who have more talent and are better drivers yet never get the opportunity to visit victory lane and be a part of that whole celebration. We also realize that winning on the racetrack came about because of the good things God had planned for us."

DALE JARRETT

"I've come to realize that there are so many bigger goals for me to set than just whether or not I win this race or a championship. It's not really whether you win or lose on the racetrack. It's whether you win or lose with the Lord."

JEFF GORDON

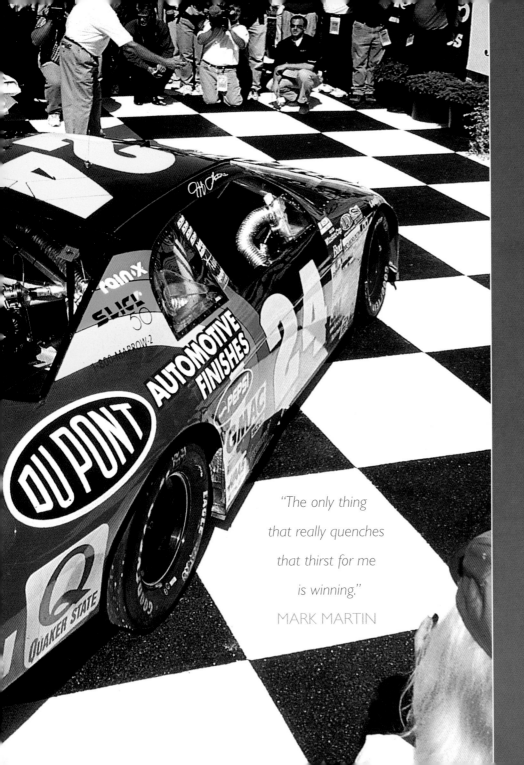

"The only thing
that really quenches
that thirst for me
is winning."

MARK MARTIN

"What we're trying to do is win championships

while honoring the Lord in doing so."

J. D. GIBBS

These men know the same is true in life. The race of life is much like that of the NASCAR driver. It is a long, often grueling challenge, fraught with sharp turns, obstacles, and even accidents. At times we run out of gas or blow a tire. There is a need for pit stops, assistance from our team, and instruction from a crew chief who sees the whole picture.

That is why so many of the champions of NASCAR have placed their trust and faith in God as their ultimate crew chief. They understand well the brevity of life and how quickly things can change. They know the only thing that matters in this race is finishing well, on the track and in life.

"I used to think that racing was everything,

but I realized as I got a little older, that's not the case.

There's a time and place for everything. There's your faith

in God, your family, and everything else. When that's

complete, then racing can complete your life."

BILL ELLIOTT

"We have a saying here at Joe Gibbs Racing. If we were going to gain from something and it's wrong, we can't do it. Yet, if we would lose by doing something and it's right, we have to do it. We want our principles to be in line with the Lord's. I would hope that people look at this race team and say, 'Hey, those guys are trying to do things the right way. There's something different there.' We want to be a witness through the way we act and the way we race."

JOE GIBBS

True champions want the wheel in their hands. But they also want to be guided by the one who will get them to the finish—the one who can tell them where they are going, how they're going to get there, where trouble might arise, and what they'll need along the way. He is their lifeline.

These men understand what it means to win in this race. This victory is forever, and in the heart of a champion, no victory is greater. Checkered flags, series titles, and trophies all pale in comparison. For in this race, the medals never tarnish, the records are never erased. All who cross the finish line are champions. To these men, this is truly what the drive to win is all about.

"My driving force is to serve God and take His message to the people who may otherwise not ever get that message. I was put here for a reason, and it wasn't just to win races."

DALE JARRETT

"There's only one guy that's going to do it out of forty-three. Everybody can't win every weekend, but when you do, it's awesome."

RANDY LAJOIE

"My driving force is Jesus Christ—

the driving force behind who I am

and what I do, how I act or how

I react, is Jesus Christ."

KYLE PETTY

*"It takes some things to happen in your life to get
close to God. But when you do, when you reach
the bottom, you start to realize there's more to it.
It makes you appreciate things, and it's certainly
made a big difference in my life."*

RAY EVERNHAM

faith
POST RACE

*"I was at the top of the world. We were winning races,
winning championships, but I had a hole in my heart.
I didn't have Jesus Christ. I'd trade the Daytona 500
and everything else for the relationship that I have
with Jesus Christ today. If it wasn't for Jesus Christ,
then where would I be?"*

DANNY MYERS

*"The way the schedules are, the way you are away from
your family, the situations you can get into both on and
off the racetrack—you have to rely on your faith."*

STEVE GRISSOM

*"Put God first. Put your family second.
And put what you want to do third."*

KYLE PETTY

*"When adversity hits in our lives, we know that if we just keep our
eyes focused on God, no matter what that mountain of adversity
is, we can look through it and focus on Him. If we go through it
the right way, then He's going to teach us things through it."*

JOE GIBBS

*"I really don't know what I would do without
the Lord in my life right now. The Lord is driving
me to be a better person. Racing is important
to me. It's an important part of my career.
But my wife and family, and my future
family, are very important to me. You have
to put all your faith in the Lord."*

JEFF GORDON

*"I had lived for racing at one time,
and now I've built my racing career on top
of an even more solid foundation than I had
fifteen years ago—being a Christian and
trying to live the way of the Bible."*

MARK MARTIN

"If you didn't have faith in God, you couldn't drive that car off in a corner like we do."
BILL ELLIOTT

"What changed my life more than anything is knowing I have God in my heart and He's on my side all the time."
DALE JARRETT

"To know that you can make a horrendous mistake and just to bow your head and close your eyes and ask for forgiveness and you see the Lord take an eraser and say, 'Okay, your slate's clean,' it's incredible to have that forgiveness."
KYLE PETTY

"Life as a Christian has its ups and downs. It's not all up by any means. But the final trip is going to be up, and that's the one that counts."
LAKE SPEED

"Maybe you've got a hole in your stomach, and you can't figure out what it is. You're not happy. Relationships fall apart. You're angry all the time. Nothing goes right. There's something missing. The best friends in the world will let you down. But Jesus Christ won't let you down. He is there all the time."
DARRELL WALTRIP

ADAM PETTY
THE HEIR

"It's something very special in our family, something that I've grown up seeing my father and my grandfather do ever since I can remember. Any kid wants to be just like their father."

ADAM PETTY, March 2000

Growing up, all that Adam Petty ever wanted to do was to race cars, following in the legacy of his father, Kyle, grandfather Richard, and great-grandfather Lee—each a NASCAR legend. At the age of nineteen, he was the first fourth-generation athlete in professional sports history and perhaps the most gifted of stock car racing's first family.

At seventeen, Adam became the youngest driver to win an American Speed Association race. A year later, he became the youngest to win an Automobile Racing Club of America race. Off the track, he displayed an easy, gregarious nature that made him a rapidly growing favorite of the media and fans alike.

And then he died.

"We're only here on earth for a short period of time. When I die and go to Heaven, that's eternity, and I want to see my wife and my kids for eternity. So we get to spend some years here on earth, who cares? Eternity is a long time. My relationship with Jesus Christ guarantees me that eternity."

KYLE PETTY, Father

"Adam loved everyone. Everyone fell in love with him. Every memory of Adam is a great memory."
MONTGOMERY LEE PETTY, Sister

"Now Adam is walking the streets with the King, asking, 'Where is the race track?' "
AUSTIN PETTY, Brother

"I think you see very few nineteen-year-olds who have touched as many people as Adam has. He was a good kid, and he always seemed to get along with everybody."
RICHARD PETTY, Grandfather

"Adam was a Christian who was always wide open, running the race to win. I think that's what Christ wants us to do. He wants us to go as hard as we can and let Him shine in our life. That's what Adam did."
COY GIBBS, Friend

Adam Petty was running a practice lap at New Hampshire International Speedway on May 12, 2000, when he hit the wall. He had only just begun his racing career. The sports world had really only just met him. Way too early, both were forced to say good-bye.

This promising young man not only emulated his father but loved and admired him in a way that was evident to all associated with the sport. "My dad's my best friend," he once told the press, a truth he need not have spoken. They all knew of the special father/son bond. After Adam's first ARCA victory, Kyle told reporters that of all the Petty clan's racing wins, this one made him the proudest. When Adam was asked about his father's words, he said, "It makes me want to cry."

Tears have been commonplace for the Petty family, and the racing family at large, at the memory of Adam. But in the midst of mourning, the Pettys found peace and even joy. They know that Adam has left them but for a short time. A few years earlier, he had emulated his father in another way: making peace with God by trusting Jesus Christ as his Savior and asking Him to guide and direct his life as Lord.

For Adam, eternity and his relationship with God took precedence over the race itself. It was Adam who called the family together nightly for a time of prayer and devotion. It was Adam who made a point each day of telling his father and mother, brother and sister, "I love you." Just prior to his death, Adam had asked Motor Racing Outreach founder and senior chaplain, Max Helton, to set up speaking engagements at churches for him. He wanted to start sharing his faith in public settings to encourage others.

Of all the great things Kyle Petty has done, no legacy will be greater than that of this son whose life served as an example of one wholly committed to God. Kyle and wife Pattie prepared their oldest son for life's most important race. Because of that, today he stands in the ultimate winner's circle, welcomed as a champion eternal.

Heart of a Champion is a registered trademark under which virtuous sports products and programs are created and distributed. Materials include award-winning videos, television and radio programs, films, books, and Internet activities. To learn more about Heart of a Champion resources, products, or programs, call 1-800-981-9298 or visit the Web site at www.heartofachampion.com.

The Heart of a Champion Foundation is an independent, national, non-profit organization utilizing the platform of sports to build and reinforce character and ethics in young people. Blending the message and the messenger, the Heart of a Champion Foundation's winning formula teaches and models character education at the grassroots level, to mold better citizens and develop the heart of a champion in youth. For more information, visit the Web site at www.heartofachampion.org. or call (972) 497-8538.

Additional copies of this book and *Passion for the Game, Inspire a Dream,* and *Above the Rim* in the *Heart of a Champion* series are available from your local bookstore.

If you have enjoyed this book or if it has impacted your life, we would like to hear from you. Please contact us at:

Honor Books
Department E
P.O. Box 55388
Tulsa, Oklahoma 74155

or by e-mail at: info@honorbooks.com

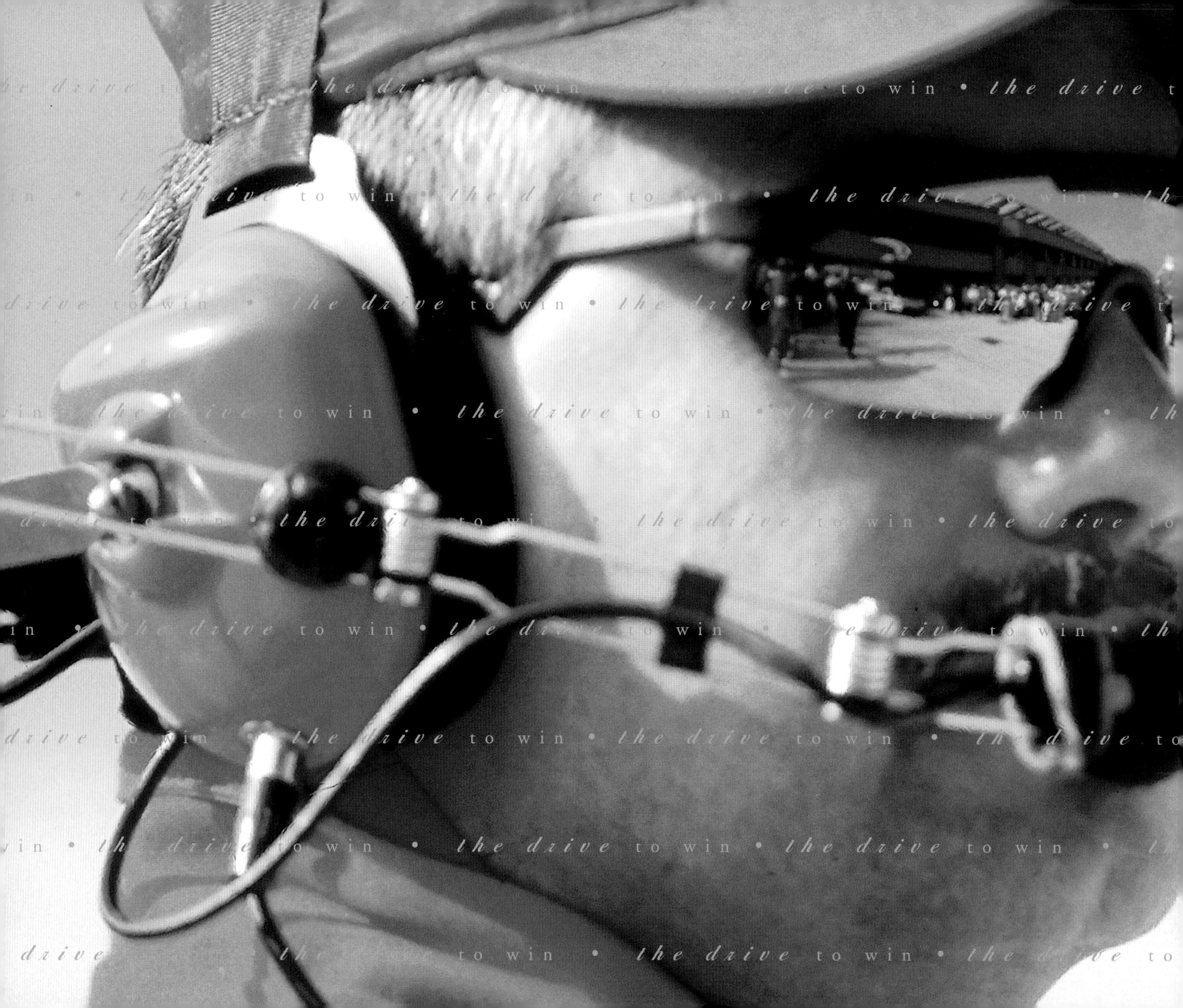
the drive to win